MAKE NOW
EAT LATER

PREP • STORE • SERVE

Publications International, Ltd.

Pictured on the front cover: Quinoa Salad with Cucumber, Tomatoes and Broccoli (*page 56*).

Pictured on the back cover (*clockwise from top left*): Key Lime Minis (*page 142*), Spring Vegetable Ragoût (*page 122*), Mixed Greens with Cranberries and Goat Cheese in a Jar (*page 36*), and Kitchen Sink Trail Mix (*page 46*).

Cover photo and photo on page 57 © Shutterstock.com

ISBN-13: 978-1-68022-895-3

Library of Congress Control Number: 2017930976

Manufactured in China.

8 7 6 5 4 3 2 1

Microwave Cooking: Microwave ovens vary in wattage. Use the cooking times as guidelines and check for doneness before adding more time.

CONTENTS

ADVANCE PREP MEALS

··

PREPARE ON THE WEEKENDS–READY TO HEAT
AND EAT DURING THE WEEK

BAKED PUMPKIN FRENCH TOAST

MAKES 6 SERVINGS

1 tablespoon butter, softened
1 loaf challah or egg bread
  (12 to 16 ounces), cut into
  ¾-inch-thick slices
7 eggs
1¼ cups whole milk
⅔ cup canned pumpkin

1 teaspoon vanilla
½ teaspoon pumpkin pie spice
⅛ teaspoon salt
3 tablespoons sugar
2 teaspoons ground cinnamon
  Maple syrup

1. Generously grease 13×9-inch baking dish with butter. Arrange bread slices in dish, fitting slices in tightly.

2. Combine eggs, milk, pumpkin, vanilla, pumpkin pie spice and salt in medium bowl; beat until well blended. Pour over bread in prepared baking dish; turn slices to coat completely with egg mixture. Cover and refrigerate 8 hours or overnight.

3. Preheat oven to 350°F. Combine sugar and cinnamon in small bowl; mix well. Turn bread slices again; sprinkle generously with cinnamon-sugar.

4. Bake about 30 minutes or until bread is puffy and golden brown. Serve immediately with maple syrup.

TIP: For a great grab-and-go breakfast, store leftover French toast in a resealable plastic container. When ready to reheat, microwave on HIGH 20 to 30 seconds. Top with maple syrup, if desired.

THAI-STYLE WARM NOODLE SALAD

MAKES 4 SERVINGS

8 ounces uncooked angel hair pasta

½ cup chunky peanut butter

¼ cup soy sauce

¼ to ½ teaspoon red pepper flakes

2 green onions, thinly sliced

1 carrot, shredded

1. Cook pasta according to package directions.

2. Meanwhile, blend peanut butter, soy sauce and red pepper flakes in serving bowl until smooth.

3. Drain pasta, reserving 5 tablespoons water. Mix hot pasta water with peanut butter mixture until smooth; toss pasta with sauce. Stir in green onions and carrot. Serve warm or at room temperature.

NOTES: This salad is as versatile as it is easy to make. It can be prepared a day ahead and served warm or cold—perfect for potlucks, picnics and even lunch boxes. You can also make it into a heartier meal by mixing in any leftover chicken or beef.

ROASTED PORK

MAKES 4 SERVINGS

3 tablespoons barbecue sauce

1 tablespoon reduced-sodium soy sauce

1 tablespoon dry sherry

2 cloves garlic, minced

½ teaspoon crushed Szechuan peppercorns or red pepper flakes

2 whole pork tenderloins (about 1¼ to 1½ pounds total)

1. Preheat oven to 350°F. Combine barbecue sauce, soy sauce, sherry, garlic and peppercorns in small bowl.

2. Brush one-fourth of mixture evenly over each roast. Place roasts on rack in shallow foil-lined roasting pan. Cook roasts 15 minutes; turn and brush with remaining barbecue sauce mixture. Continue to cook until internal temperature reaches 165°F when tested with meat thermometer inserted in thickest part of roast. (Timing will depend on thickness of pork; test at 30 minutes.)

3. Transfer roast to cutting board; cover with foil. Let stand 10 to 15 minutes before carving. Internal temperature will continue to rise 5° to 10°F during stand time. Slice diagonally and serve warm with rice, if desired. Or, for use in other recipes, cut into portions and refrigerate up to 3 days or freeze up to 3 months.

VARIATION: For Chinese Barbecued Pork, add 1 teaspoon red food coloring to barbecue sauce mixture. Prepare roasts as recipe directs. Roasts can be grilled over medium coals until an internal temperature of 155°F is reached. (Turn pork after 8 minutes; check temperature at 16 minutes.)

TURKEY PASTA WITH SOUR CREAM AND PARMESAN

MAKES 4 SERVINGS

6 ounces uncooked multigrain vermicelli, broken in half, or penne or rotini pasta

2 ounces cream cheese

½ cup sour cream

¼ cup milk

2 medium cloves garlic, minced

½ teaspoon salt (optional)

2 cups diced cooked turkey

½ cup frozen (or leftover) green peas

1 jar (2 ounces) diced pimientos, drained

¼ cup plus 2 tablespoons chopped green onions, divided

¼ cup grated Parmesan cheese

¼ teaspoon black pepper

⅛ teaspoon salt

1. Cook vermicelli according to package directions. Drain; return to pan. Cover to keep warm.

2. Meanwhile, microwave cream cheese in medium microwavable bowl on HIGH 20 seconds or until softened. Whisk in sour cream, milk, garlic and salt, if desired.

3. Add turkey and peas to hot vermicelli; let stand 1 minute. Meanwhile, microwave cream cheese mixture on HIGH 1 minute or until heated through.

4. Transfer vermicelli mixture to serving dish. Add pimientos, ¼ cup green onions, cheese, pepper and salt; mix well. Fold in cream cheese mixture until evenly coated. Sprinkle with remaining 2 tablespoons green onions.

TIP: Make a day ahead for best flavor.

HURRIED HEARTY SKILLET BEEF AND RICE

MAKES 4 SERVINGS

1 cup uncooked instant or converted rice

½ teaspoon ground turmeric (optional)

1 pound lean ground beef

1½ cups mild, medium or hot salsa

½ cup frozen corn kernels

1 teaspoon beef bouillon granules

1 teaspoon ground cumin, plus more to taste

1½ teaspoons sugar

Sour cream (optional)

1. Cook rice according to directions on package, adding turmeric, if desired.

2. Meanwhile, place large skillet over medium-high heat until hot. Add ground beef; cook until browned, stirring frequently. Add all remaining ingredients except sour cream. Bring to a boil, reduce heat, cover tightly and simmer 5 minutes or until thickened slightly. Add more cumin, if desired.

3. Serve over cooked rice and top with sour cream, if desired.

VARIATION: For chili, omit rice. Add 1 can (14½ ounces) diced tomatoes and 1 can (15½ ounces) dark red kidney beans, rinsed and drained.

TIP: This dish freezes well, so make a double batch and freeze half. Do not freeze rice.

FRIED RICE WITH SHRIMP

MAKES 6 SERVINGS

2 tablespoons vegetable oil

3 green onions, chopped

2 eggs lightly beaten

3 cups cooked rice, chilled or at room temperature

¼ pound cooked shrimp, chopped

3 tablespoons low-sodium soy sauce

1. Heat wok or large skillet over medium heat. Add oil; heat until oil shimmers. Add green onions; cook and stir about 30 seconds. Pour in eggs, stirring constantly until cooked.

2. Add rice; cook and stir 2 to 3 minutes or until heated through. Stir in shrimp and soy sauce; cook and stir 1 to 2 minutes or until heated through.

VARIATION: If you don't have shrimp on hand, you can substitute cooked ham, beef, pork or chicken instead. Or, experiment by substituting cooked vegetables, such as peas, carrots or broccoli.

TIP: Making fried rice is a great way to use up leftover rice. In fact, when you're cooking rice, plan ahead and make extra rice to chill for fried rice dishes.

LASAGNA SUPREME

MAKES 8 TO 10 SERVINGS

8 ounces uncooked lasagna noodles

½ pound mild Italian sausage, casings removed

½ pound ground beef

1 medium onion, chopped

2 cloves garlic, minced

1 can (about 14 ounces) whole tomatoes, undrained and chopped

1 can (6 ounces) tomato paste

2 teaspoons dried basil

1 teaspoon dried marjoram

1 can (4 ounces) sliced mushrooms, drained

2 eggs

2 cups (16 ounces) cottage cheese

¾ cup grated Parmesan cheese, divided

2 tablespoons dried parsley flakes

½ teaspoon salt

½ teaspoon black pepper

2 cups (8 ounces) shredded Cheddar cheese

3 cups (12 ounces) shredded mozzarella cheese

1. Cook lasagna noodles according to package directions. Drain; cover and keep warm.

2. Brown sausage, ground beef, onion and garlic in large skillet over medium-high heat, stirring to break up meat; drain fat.

3. Add tomatoes with juice, tomato paste, basil and marjoram. Reduce heat to low. Cover; simmer 15 minutes, stirring often. Stir in mushrooms; set aside.

4. Preheat oven to 375°F. Beat eggs in large bowl; add cottage cheese, ½ cup Parmesan cheese, parsley flakes, salt and pepper. Mix well.

5. Place half of noodles in bottom of greased 13×9-inch baking pan. Spread half of cottage cheese mixture over noodles, then half of meat mixture, half of Cheddar cheese and half of mozzarella cheese. Repeat layers. Top with remaining ¼ cup Parmesan cheese.

6. Bake 40 to 45 minutes or until hot and bubbly. Let stand 10 minutes before cutting.

TIP: Lasagna can be assembled, covered and refrigerated up to 2 days in advance. Bake, uncovered, in preheated 375°F oven 60 minutes or until hot and bubbly.

CRISPY ROASTED CHICKEN

MAKES 8 TO 10 SERVINGS

1 roasting chicken or capon
  (about 6½ pounds)
1 tablespoon peanut or
  vegetable oil

2 cloves garlic, minced
1 tablespoon soy sauce

1. Preheat oven to 350°F. Place on rack in shallow, foil-lined roasting pan.

2. Combine oil and garlic in small cup; brush evenly over chicken. Roast 15 to 20 minutes per pound or until internal temperature reaches 170°F when tested meat thermometer inserted in thickest part of thigh not touching bone.

3. *Increase oven temperature to 450°F.* Remove drippings from pan; discard. Brush chicken evenly with soy sauce. Roast 5 to 10 minutes until skin is very crisp and deep golden brown. Transfer chicken to cutting board; let stand 10 to 15 minutes before carving. Internal temperature will continue to rise 5° to 10°F during stand time. Cover and refrigerate leftovers up to 3 days or freeze up to 3 months.

BAKED VEGETABLE PENNE

MAKES 6 SERVINGS

6 ounces (about 2 cups) uncooked whole wheat penne or ziti pasta

1 large zucchini

1 yellow squash

1 red onion

1 red bell pepper

1 tablespoon canola oil

2 cups sliced mushrooms

1 teaspoon salt

1 teaspoon dried Italian seasoning

½ cup part-skim ricotta cheese

2 cups pasta sauce, divided

½ cup shredded part-skim mozzarella cheese

2 tablespoons shredded Parmesan cheese (optional)

1. Preheat oven to 400°F. Spray 11×7-inch baking dish with nonstick cooking spray. Cook penne according to package directions. Drain and return to saucepan; keep warm.

2. Cut zucchini, yellow squash and red onion with fine spiral blade of spiralizer. Cut bell pepper with spiral slice blade.* Cut vegetables into desired lengths.

3. Heat oil in large nonstick skillet over medium-high heat. Add mushrooms; cook and stir 2 to 3 minutes or until mushrooms are browned. Stir in zucchini, yellow squash, onion, bell pepper, salt and Italian seasoning. Remove from heat.

4. Add ricotta cheese and 1½ cups pasta sauce to penne. Spread half of mixture into prepared baking dish. Layer with vegetable mixture, remaining penne mixture, pasta sauce and mozzarella cheese.

5. Bake 20 minutes or until cheese is melted with some brown spots. Let stand 15 minutes before serving. Sprinkle with Parmesan cheese, if desired.

*If you do not have a spiralizer, thinly slice vegetables.

NOTE: This dish can be assembled, covered and refrigerated up to 2 days in advance. Bake, uncovered, in preheated 400°F oven 20 to 25 minutes or until heated through.

PIZZA TURNOVERS

MAKES 6 SERVINGS

5 ounces reduced-fat mild Italian turkey sausage	1 package (about 14 ounces) refrigerated pizza dough
½ cup pizza sauce	⅓ cup shredded reduced-fat Italian cheese blend

1. Preheat oven to 425°F. Line baking sheet with parchment paper or spray with olive oil cooking spray.

2. Brown sausage in medium nonstick skillet over medium heat, stirring to break up meat. Drain fat. Add pizza sauce; cook and stir until heated through.

3. Unroll pizza dough on prepared baking sheet; pat into 12×8-inch rectangle. Cut into 6 (4-inch) squares. Divide sausage mixture evenly among squares. Sprinkle with cheese. Fold dough over filling to form triangles. Press edges with fork to seal.

4. Bake 11 to 13 minutes or until golden brown. Serve warm or cool on wire rack and freeze.

TIP: To freeze turnovers, remove to wire rack to cool 30 minutes. Individually wrap in plastic wrap; place in freezer container or resealable freezer bag and freeze. To reheat turnovers, preheat oven to 400°F. Place turnovers in ungreased baking pan; cover loosely with foil. Bake 18 to 22 minutes or until heated through. Or, place one turnover on a paper towel-lined microwavable plate. Microwave on LOW (30%) 3 to 3½ minutes or until heated through, turning once.

TURKEY AND VEGGIE MEATBALLS WITH FENNEL

MAKES 6 SERVINGS

1 pound lean ground turkey

½ cup finely chopped green onions

½ cup finely chopped green bell pepper

⅓ cup old-fashioned oats

¼ cup shredded carrot

¼ cup grated Parmesan cheese

2 egg whites

2 cloves garlic, minced

½ teaspoon Italian seasoning

¼ teaspoon fennel seeds

¼ teaspoon salt

⅛ teaspoon red pepper flakes (optional)

1 teaspoon extra virgin olive oil

1. Combine all ingredients except oil in large bowl; mix well. Shape mixture into 36 (1-inch) balls.

2. Heat oil in large nonstick skillet over medium-high heat. Add meatballs; cook 11 minutes or until no longer pink in center, turning frequently. Use fork and spoon for easy turning. Serve immediately or cool and freeze.*

*To freeze, cool completely and place in gallon-size resealable food storage bag. Release any excess air from bag and seal. Freeze bag flat for easier storage and faster thawing. This will also allow you to remove as many meatballs as needed without them sticking together. To reheat, place meatballs in a 12×8-inch microwavable dish and cook on HIGH 20 to 30 seconds or until hot.

BAKED PASTA CASSEROLE

MAKES 2 SERVINGS

1½ cups (3 ounces) uncooked wagon wheel (rotelle) pasta

3 ounces 95% lean ground beef

2 tablespoons chopped onion

2 tablespoons chopped green bell pepper

1 clove garlic, minced

½ cup pasta sauce

Dash black pepper

2 tablespoons shredded Italian-style mozzarella and Parmesan cheese blend

Pepperoncini (optional)

1. Preheat oven to 350°F. Cook pasta according to package directions, omitting salt. Drain; return pasta to saucepan.

2. Meanwhile, heat medium nonstick skillet over medium-high heat. Add beef, onion, bell pepper and garlic; cook and stir 3 to 4 minutes or until beef is no longer pink and vegetables are crisp-tender. Drain.

3. Add beef mixture, pasta sauce and black pepper to pasta in saucepan; mix well. Spoon mixture into 1-quart baking dish. Sprinkle with cheese.

4. Bake 15 minutes or until heated through. Serve with pepperoncini, if desired.

NOTE: To make ahead, assemble casserole as directed above through step 3. Cover and refrigerate several hours or overnight. Bake, uncovered, in preheated 350°F oven 30 minutes or until heated through.

OVERNIGHT CHEESY VEGETABLE STRATA

MAKES 10 SERVINGS

5 cups whole grain bread cubes

2 cups cooked broccoli, coarsely chopped

1 cup cooked mushrooms, chopped

½ cup sliced green onions

1¼ cups (5 ounces) shredded Swiss cheese, divided

2 cups cholesterol-free egg substitute

2 cups fat-free (skim) milk

1 tablespoon Dijon mustard

½ teaspoon black pepper

¼ teaspoon salt

1. Layer bread, broccoli, mushrooms and green onions in greased 13×9 baking dish. Sprinkle ¾ cup cheese evenly over vegetables.

2. Whisk egg substitute, milk, mustard, pepper and salt in medium bowl. Pour over strata. Refrigerate, covered, overnight.

3. Preheat oven to 350°F. Bake, uncovered, 30 minutes.

4. Sprinkle remaining ½ cup cheese evenly over top. Bake 10 to 12 minutes or until knife inserted into center comes out clean. Let stand 10 minutes before cutting and serving.

SPICY LASAGNA ROLLERS

MAKES 12 SERVINGS

1½ pounds Italian sausage, casings removed

1 jar (26 ounces) pasta sauce, divided

1 can (8 ounces) tomato sauce

½ cup chopped roasted red pepper

¾ teaspoon Italian seasoning

½ teaspoon red pepper flakes

1 container (15 ounces) ricotta cheese

1 package (10 ounces) frozen chopped spinach, thawed and squeezed dry

2 cups (8 ounces) shredded Italian cheese blend, divided

1 cup (4 ounces) shredded Cheddar cheese, divided

1 egg, lightly beaten

12 lasagna noodles, cooked and drained

1. Preheat oven to 350°F. Spray 13×9-inch baking pan with nonstick cooking spray.

2. Brown sausage in large skillet over medium heat, stirring to break up meat; drain fat. Stir in ½ cup pasta sauce, tomato sauce, roasted red pepper, Italian seasoning and red pepper flakes.

3. Combine ricotta cheese, spinach, 1½ cups Italian cheese blend, ½ cup Cheddar cheese and egg in medium bowl. Spread ¼ cup ricotta mixture over each noodle. Top with ⅓ cup sausage mixture. Tightly roll up each noodle from short end. Place rolls, seam side down, in prepared baking pan. Pour remaining pasta sauce over rolls. Sprinkle with remaining ½ cup Italian cheese blend and ½ cup Cheddar cheese. Cover with foil.*

4. Bake 30 minutes. Remove foil; bake 15 minutes or until sauce is bubbly.

If you prefer, assemble rollers to this point, cover and refrigerate several hours or overnight. Bake in preheated 350°F oven 30 to 35 minutes or until heated through.

MAKE IT & TAKE IT

PACK IT UP AND TAKE IT ON THE GO

CHOPPED SALAD

MAKES 4 (1-QUART) SERVINGS

2 tablespoons fresh lemon juice

2 tablespoons fresh lime juice

1 tablespoon creamy peanut butter

1 tablespoon sugar

1 teaspoon sesame seeds

½ teaspoon minced garlic

¼ teaspoon black pepper

1 cup cooked turkey breast, chopped

2 cups chopped romaine lettuce

3 cups baby spinach, chopped

½ head bok choy, chopped

½ cup baby carrots, chopped

½ cup sugar snap peas, chopped

1 small tomato, chopped

1. Combine lemon juice, lime juice, peanut butter, sugar, sesame seeds, garlic and pepper in small jar with tight fitting lid. Shake well until distributed. Pour into 4 (½-cup) resealable containers.

2. Layer turkey, romaine, spinach, bok choy, carrots, snap peas and tomato in 4 (1-quart) jars. Seal jars. Refrigerate until ready to take or serve. Serve with dressing.

SPICY NUTS 'N' CRANBERRIES MIX

MAKES 1 (1-QUART) JAR

¼ cup granulated brown sugar*

½ teaspoon salt

½ teaspoon chipotle chili powder *or* ground red pepper

2¼ cups pecan halves

¾ cup dried cranberries

1 cup whole almonds

Granulated brown sugar is brown sugar that has been processed to have a light, dry texture similar to granulated sugar. It can be found in the baking aisle of most supermarkets.

1. Combine brown sugar, salt and chili powder in small bowl; mix well. Pour into 1-quart wide-mouth jar with tight-fitting lid. Add ¾ cup pecans, cranberries, ¾ cup pecans, ½ cup almonds, remaining ¾ cup pecans and ½ cup almonds. Pack down firmly after each layer. Seal jar.

2. Prepare Spicy Nuts 'n' Cranberries by following the instructions listed below.

SPICY NUTS 'N' CRANBERRIES

MAKES ABOUT 4 CUPS

1 jar Spicy Nuts 'n' Cranberries Mix

¼ cup (½ stick) butter

¼ cup maple syrup

1. Preheat oven to 325°F. Line large baking sheet with heavy-duty foil; generously grease foil. Pour contents of jar into large bowl; mix well.

2. Combine butter and maple syrup in large nonstick saucepan; heat over low heat until butter melts, stirring constantly. Stir in nut mixture. Remove from heat; stir until mixture is well coated. Spread evenly on prepared baking sheet.

3. Bake 20 to 25 minutes or until nuts are fragrant and golden brown, stirring every 10 minutes. (Mixture will be saucy; glaze will firm up as nuts cool.) Cool completely on baking sheet, stirring occasionally to separate into small pieces. Store in airtight container.

MIXED GREENS WITH CRANBERRIES AND GOAT CHEESE IN A JAR

MAKES 2 (1-QUART) SERVINGS

¼ cup vegetable oil

2 tablespoons soy sauce

1½ tablespoons balsamic vinegar

1 tablespoon packed dark brown sugar

1 teaspoon grated fresh ginger

½ teaspoon red pepper flakes

½ cup chopped toasted pecans*

⅔ cup dried cranberries

⅔ cup finely chopped red onion

⅔ cup crumbled goat cheese

3 cups baby spring salad greens mix

To toast pecans, spread in a single layer on ungreased baking sheet. Bake in preheated 350°F oven 8 to 10 minutes or until fragrant, stirring occasionally.

1. Whisk oil, soy sauce, vinegar, brown sugar, ginger and red pepper flakes in small jar. Secure lid and shake vigorously until well blended. Pour equal amounts dressing into bottom of 2 (1-quart) resealable jars.

2. Layer pecans, cranberries, onion, goat cheese and salad greens in jars; seal jars. Refrigerate until ready to take or serve.

CHEESE IN A JAR

MAKES 8 SERVINGS

1 pound (16 ounces) feta cheese, cubed

½ cup extra virgin olive oil

2 tablespoons finely minced green bell pepper

2 tablespoons finely minced red bell pepper

2 to 3 cloves garlic, finely minced

1 tablespoon chopped Italian parsley *or* 1 teaspoon dried parsley flakes

2 teaspoons fresh rosemary leaves *or* 1 teaspoon dried rosemary

1 teaspoon peppercorns

½ teaspoon red pepper flakes

¼ teaspoon salt

¼ teaspoon black pepper

1. Place all ingredients in clean, dry, large glass jar with tight-fitting lid. Marinate in refrigerator several hours or up to several days. Flip jar upside-down occasionally to immerse cheese in seasonings and oil.

2. Serve with toasted baguette slices, crackers, fruit or vegetables, if desired. As cheese is used up, additional cubed cheese can be added to jar, or remaining herb-oil mixture can be made into vinaigrette dressing by adding vinegar to the jar. Shake jar before serving.

AVOCADO GARDEN MINIS

MAKES 6 SERVINGS

1 package (3 ounces) oriental-flavored ramen noodles

1 ripe medium avocado, diced

3 tablespoons finely chopped red onion

1 cup grape tomatoes, quartered

¾ cup diced peeled cucumber

¼ cup chopped fresh cilantro

¼ cup plus 2 tablespoons extra virgin olive oil

2 tablespoons lemon juice

2 medium cloves garlic, minced

¼ teaspoon salt

⅛ teaspoon black pepper

1. Break noodles into 4 pieces. Cook according to package directions using seasoning packet; drain well. Cool to room temperature.

2. Spoon equal parts of noodles, avocado, onion, tomatoes, cucumber and cilantro into 6 mini mason jars or small ramekins.

3. Whisk oil, lemon juice, garlic, salt and pepper in small bowl until well blended. Drizzle dressing over each salad. Refrigerate 10 minutes to allow flavors to blend.

PEANUTTY HAM TURNOVERS

MAKES 8 SERVINGS

8 ounces finely diced cooked ham (about 2 cups)

1 cup (4 ounces) shredded Monterey Jack cheese

¼ cup chopped roasted salted peanuts

3 tablespoons orange marmalade

2 tablespoons dried currants

1 to 1¼ teaspoons medium-hot chili powder

1 package (about 16 ounces) refrigerated jumbo buttermilk biscuits (8 biscuits)

1. Preheat oven to 350°F. Line baking sheet with parchment paper.

2. Combine ham, cheese, peanuts, marmalade, currants and chili powder to taste in medium bowl; mix well.

3. Separate biscuits; roll out each biscuit into 6-inch circle on lightly floured surface. Spoon about ⅓ cup filling into center of each biscuit. Fold biscuit over filling to form semicircle; press edges to seal tightly. Crimp edges, if desired. Place on prepared baking sheet.

4. Bake 15 minutes or until biscuits are golden brown and filling is heated through. Serve warm or at room temperature.

NOTE: Refrigerate extra turnovers for 2 days or freeze up to 1 month. Place in individual resealable food storage bags for storage and packing.

TIP: These turnovers are good hot or cold. To keep turnovers cool in a lunch box, include a frozen juice box or frozen gel pack. Reheat turnovers in the microwave, if desired.

GREEK PASTA SALAD IN A JAR

MAKES 6 (1-PINT) SERVINGS

PASTA SALAD

- 6 cups cooked regular or multigrain rotini pasta
- 1½ cups diced cucumber
- 1 cup diced tomatoes (about 2 medium)
- 1 cup diced green bell pepper (about 1 medium)
- 1 package (4 ounces) crumbled feta cheese
- 12 medium pitted black olives, sliced
- ¼ cup chopped fresh dill

DRESSING

- ¼ cup olive oil
- ¼ cup lemon juice
- ¼ teaspoon salt
- ¼ teaspoon dried oregano
- ⅛ teaspoon black pepper

1. Combine all pasta salad ingredients in large bowl.

2. Combine dressing ingredients in small bowl. Pour over salad; toss well.

3. Spoon about 2 cups pasta salad into each of 6 (1-pint) resealable jars. Seal jars. Refrigerate until ready to take or serve.

KITCHEN SINK TRAIL MIX

MAKES 1 (1-QUART) JAR

1 to 1¼ cups granola cereal, divided

½ cup raisins

½ cup red and green mini candy-coated chocolate pieces*

⅓ cup shredded sweetened coconut

¼ cup slivered almonds, toasted**

¼ cup chopped dried apricots***

¼ cup roasted salted green or white pumpkin seeds

¼ cup coarsely chopped pecans, toasted**

¼ cup coarsely chopped dried cranberries***

¼ cup peanut butter chips

¼ cup white chocolate chips

1 teaspoon ground cinnamon

⅓ teaspoon ground cardamom

Or substitute multicolored candy-coated chocolate pieces.
**To toast nuts, spread in single layer in small heavy skillet. Cook over medium heat 1 to 2 minutes, stirring frequently, or until lightly browned. Remove from skillet immediately. Cool before using.*
***Spray knife with nonstick cooking spray to prevent sticking.*

Layer all ingredients, except cinnamon and cardamom, in 1-quart wide-mouth jar with tight-fitting lid. Use ¼-cup portions of granola to separate layers (save any excess granola for another use). Pack down firmly after each layer. Blend cinnamon and cardamom in small resealable food storage bag; place in jar. Seal jar.

KITCHEN SINK TRAIL MIX: Remove bag from jar. Pour remaining contents of jar into large bowl; stir well. Add contents of bag; stir until evenly blended. Store in airtight container.

COBB SALAD TO GO

MAKES 4 (1-QUART) SERVINGS

½ cup blue cheese salad dressing

1 ripe avocado, diced

1 tomato, chopped

6 ounces cooked chicken breast, cut into bite-size pieces

4 slices bacon, crisp-cooked and crumbled *or* ½ cup bacon bits

2 hard cooked eggs, mashed

1 large carrot, shredded

½ cup blue cheese, crumbled

1 package (10 ounces) torn mixed salad greens

1. Place 2 tablespoons salad dressing into bottom of 4 (1-quart) jars. Layer in the following order: avocado, tomato, chicken, bacon, eggs, carrot, blue cheese and salad greens. Seal jars.

2. Refrigerate until ready to take or serve.

WHAT A GRAPE SALAD

MAKES 4 SERVINGS

1½ cups green and/or red seedless grapes, halved

1 red apple (such as Gala, Jonathon or Braeburn), cored and diced

½ cup finely diced celery

1 tablespoon golden raisins

½ cup mayonnaise

2 tablespoons yogurt

2 tablespoons crushed cereal

Place grapes, apple, celery and raisins in medium bowl. Mix mayonnaise and yogurt in small bowl. Gently stir into grape mixture. (Salad may be made up to 1 day ahead. Seal in airtight container and refrigerate until serving time.) Sprinkle each serving with cereal.

TAKE-ALONG ITALIAN BREAD SALAD

MAKES 4 (1-PINT) SERVINGS

4 slices Italian bread, cut into ½-inch cubes (about 4 cups)

½ cup low-fat buttermilk

1 clove garlic, minced

1 tablespoon minced fresh dill *or* 1 teaspoon dried dill weed

1½ teaspoons onion powder

¼ teaspoon salt, plus additional as needed

¼ teaspoon black pepper

½ cup heirloom medley cherry tomatoes, quartered

1 cucumber, peeled, cut lengthwise into halves, seeded and thinly sliced

1 stalk celery, thinly sliced

2 tablespoons minced fresh basil

1. Preheat oven to 400°F. Place bread on baking sheet. Bake 5 to 7 minutes or until lightly toasted and dry, stirring occasionally. Remove from pan; let cool.

2. Combine buttermilk, garlic, dill, onion powder, ¼ teaspoon salt and pepper in small bowl; mix well. Let stand 15 minutes to allow flavors to blend.

3. Spoon equal amounts bread cubes into bottom of 4 (1-pint) resealable jars. Layer tomatoes, cucumber, celery and basil over top of bread. Sprinkle with additional salt, if desired.

4. Mix dressing. Pour equal amounts over salad. Shake jars to distribute dressing. Refrigerate until ready to take or serve.

MARINATED BEAN AND VEGETABLE SALAD

MAKES 8 SERVINGS

¼ cup orange juice

3 tablespoons white wine vinegar

1 tablespoon canola or vegetable oil

2 cloves garlic, minced

1 can (about 15 ounces) Great Northern beans, rinsed and drained

1 can (about 15 ounces) kidney beans, rinsed and drained

¼ cup coarsely chopped red cabbage

¼ cup chopped red onion

¼ cup chopped green bell pepper

¼ cup chopped red bell pepper

¼ cup sliced celery

1. Combine orange juice, vinegar, oil and garlic in small jar with tight-fitting lid; shake well.

2. Combine beans, cabbage, onion, bell peppers and celery in large bowl. Pour dressing over bean mixture; toss to coat.

3. Refrigerate, covered, 1 to 2 hours to allow flavors to blend. Toss before serving.

QUINOA SALAD WITH CUCUMBER, TOMATOES AND BROCCOLI

MAKES 3 (1-PINT) SERVINGS

½ cup quinoa

1 cup water

1 cup diced cucumber

1 cup cherry tomatoes, halved

1 cup fresh broccoli florets

½ cup shredded carrots

2 green onions, minced

¼ cup roughly chopped fresh parsley

3 tablespoons extra virgin olive oil

1 tablespoon red wine vinegar

½ teaspoon kosher salt

¼ teaspoon black pepper

1. Place quinoa in fine-mesh strainer; rinse well under cold running water. Bring 1 cup water to a boil in small saucepan; stir. Reduce heat to low; cover and simmer 6 minutes or until quinoa is tender and water is absorbed. Cool completely.

2. Layer cucumber, quinoa, tomatoes, broccoli, carrots, green onions and parsley in 3 (1-pint) resealable jars.

3. Combine oil, vinegar, salt and pepper in small bowl; mix well. Top salad evenly with dressing. Seal jars; shake to distribute dressing.

4. Refrigerate until ready to take or serve.

GAME DAY SNACK MIX

MAKES 1 (1-QUART) JAR

- ½ cup packed brown sugar
- 1 teaspoon medium-hot chili powder
- ½ teaspoon salt
- ½ teaspoon curry powder
- ½ teaspoon Chinese five-spice powder
- 1½ cups raw almonds
- 1 cup dried cherries
- 1 cup shelled raw pistachio nuts

1. Combine brown sugar, chili powder, salt, curry powder and five-spice powder in medium bowl; stir well. Layer brown sugar mixture, almonds, cherries and pistachios in 1-quart jar with tight-fitting lid. Pack ingredients down lightly before adding each layer. Seal jar.

2. Prepare Game Day Snack Mix by following the instructions listed below.

GAME DAY SNACK

MAKES 14 (¼-CUP) SERVINGS

- 1 egg white
- 1 jar Game Day Snack Mix

1. Preheat oven to 250°F.

2. Whisk egg white in large bowl until frothy. Add contents of jar; stir gently to coat with egg white.

3. Spread mixture evenly onto nonstick baking sheet. Bake 35 to 40 minutes, stirring occasionally. Let mixture cool 30 minutes or until coating is firm. Break into small chunks. Store mix in airtight container.

APPLE AND CHEESE POCKETS

MAKES 8 SERVINGS

2 cups Golden Delicious apples, peeled, cored and finely chopped (about 2 medium)

2 cups (8 ounces) shredded sharp Cheddar cheese

2 tablespoons apple jelly

¼ teaspoon curry powder

1 package (about 16 ounces) large reduced-fat refrigerated biscuits (8 biscuits)

1. Preheat oven to 350°F. Line baking sheet with parchment paper; set aside.

2. Combine apples, cheese, jelly and curry powder in large bowl; stir well.

3. Roll out 1 biscuit on lightly floured surface to 6½-inch circle. Place ½ cup apple mixture in center. Fold biscuit over filling to form semicircle; press to seal tightly. Place on prepared baking sheet. Repeat with remaining biscuits and filling. Bake 15 to 18 minutes or until biscuits are golden and filling is heated through.

TIP: Refrigerate leftovers up to 2 days or freeze up to 1 month. To reheat thawed pockets, microwave about 30 seconds on HIGH or until heated through.

TAKE A TACO SALAD TO WORK

MAKES 4 (1-QUART) JARS

DRESSING

- ¼ cup mayonnaise
- ¼ cup plain yogurt *or* sour cream
- 1 tablespoon lime juice
- ½ teaspoon chipotle chili powder
- 1 clove garlic, minced
- ¼ cup crumbled cotija cheese
- ¼ cup chopped fresh cilantro

SALAD

- 1 tablespoon vegetable oil
- 1 package (16 ounces) frozen corn
- ¼ teaspoon salt
- 1 large avocado, diced
- 1 teaspoon lime juice
- 1 can (about 15 ounces) black beans, rinsed and drained
- 2 medium tomatoes, seeded and diced (1 cup)
- ½ cup finely chopped red onion
- Packaged tortilla chips
- Chopped fresh spinach *or* lettuce

1. For dressing, whisk mayonnaise, yogurt, 1 tablespoon lime juice, chili powder and garlic in small bowl. Stir in cheese and cilantro.

2. Heat oil in saucepan over high heat. Add corn; cook 10 to 15 minutes or until lightly browned, stirring occasionally. Stir in salt. Transfer to medium bowl; cool to room temperature. Combine avocado and 1 teaspoon lime juice in small bowl; toss to coat.

3. For each jar, layer 2½ tablespoons dressing, ½ cup corn, scant ½ cup black beans, ¼ cup tomatoes, 2 tablespoons onion and about ¼ cup avocado. Top with tortilla chips and lettuce.

NOTE: You can also make these without the lettuce. If so, use 4 (1-pint) jars.

STAPLES TO THE RESCUE

WITH A FEW ITEMS, AND YOUR PANTRY STAPLES, YOU'LL HAVE WEEKNIGHT MEALS IN NO TIME

CASHEW CHICKEN

MAKES 4 SERVINGS

1 pound boneless skinless chicken breasts or thighs

2 teaspoons minced fresh ginger

1 tablespoon peanut or vegetable oil

1 medium red bell pepper, cut into short, thin strips

⅓ cup teriyaki sauce

⅓ cup roasted or dry roasted cashews

Hot cooked rice (optional)

Coarsely chopped fresh cilantro (optional)

1. Cut chicken into ½-inch slices; cut each slice into 1½-inch strips. Toss chicken with ginger in small bowl.

2. Heat oil in wok or large skillet over medium-high heat. Add chicken mixture; stir-fry 2 minutes. Add bell pepper; stir-fry 4 minutes or until chicken is cooked through.

3. Add teriyaki sauce; stir-fry 1 minute or until sauce is heated through. Stir in cashews. Serve over rice, if desired. Garnish with cilantro.

STIR-FRY VEGETABLE PIZZA

MAKES 4 SERVINGS

1 pound (about 5 cups) fresh cut stir-fry vegetables (packaged or from the salad bar) such as broccoli, zucchini, bell peppers and red onions

1 (12-inch) prepared pizza crust

⅓ cup pizza sauce

¼ teaspoon red pepper flakes (optional)

1½ cups (6 ounces) shredded part-skim mozzarella cheese

1. Heat oven to 425°F.

2. Heat large nonstick skillet over medium-high heat 1 minute; coat with nonstick cooking spray. Add vegetables; stir-fry 4 to 5 minutes or until crisp-tender.

3. Place pizza crust on large baking sheet; top with pizza sauce. Sprinkle red pepper flakes over sauce, if desired. Arrange vegetables over sauce; top with cheese.

4. Bake 12 to 14 minutes or until crust is golden brown and cheese is melted. Cut into 8 wedges.

FOCACCIA BARS

MAKES 4 SERVINGS

Cornmeal

1 package (11 ounces) refrigerated French bread dough

2 tablespoons olive oil

1 large red or yellow bell pepper, thinly sliced

¼ teaspoon coarse salt

⅛ teaspoon dried oregano

¼ cup (1 ounce) shredded Italian cheese blend

1. Preheat oven to 400°F. Sprinkle cornmeal on baking sheet. Shape dough into 16×4-inch rectangle on prepared baking sheet.

2. Heat oil in medium skillet over medium-high heat. Add bell pepper; cook and stir 3 to 5 minutes or until pepper is tender and lightly browned. Remove from skillet, reserving oil.

3. Press fingertips into dough to create dimples. Drizzle leftover oil from skillet onto dough. Spread pepper slices over dough. Sprinkle with salt and oregano. Top with cheese.

4. Bake 13 to 15 minutes or until cheese melts and bread is golden brown. Let focaccia rest 2 to 3 minutes. Cut into 4 (4-inch) squares. Serve warm or at room temperature.

NOTE: Refrigerate leftovers up to 2 days or freeze up to 1 month.

GRILLED WASABI FLANK STEAK

MAKES 2 SERVINGS

6 tablespoons wasabi horseradish

2 tablespoons olive oil

1 beef flank steak (1 to 1½ pounds)

2 large red potatoes, cut into ¼-inch-thick slices

¼ cup water

1 teaspoon salt

1. Combine horseradish and oil in small bowl. Spread 2 tablespoons mixture on both sides of steak. Marinate in refrigerator 30 minutes or up to 2 hours.

2. Place potatoes, water and salt in microwavable dish; cover and microwave on HIGH 5 minutes. Drain potatoes. Add 2 tablespoons horseradish mixture; toss to coat.

3. Prepare grill for direct cooking.

4. Grill steak, covered, over medium heat 8 minutes; turn. Place potatoes on grid. Brush potatoes; then steak with remaining horseradish mixture. Grill 8 to 10 minutes or until steak is medium rare (145°F) and potatoes are slightly browned. Season with salt, if desired.

SALMON IN THE WILD

MAKES 4 SERVINGS

1 package (6 ounces) long grain and wild rice mix

1 tablespoon butter or margarine, cut into small pieces

½ cup shredded carrot

2 cups boiling water

1 pound salmon fillets, skin removed

⅓ cup teriyaki sauce

1 sliced orange (optional)

1. Preheat oven to 350°F. Pour rice and contents of seasoning packet into 8-inch square baking dish. Dot top of rice with butter and top with carrot. Pour boiling water into baking dish.

2. Cut salmon into 8 pieces and evenly space on top of rice mixture. Cover dish with foil and bake 20 minutes. Remove foil; bake 5 minutes longer.

3. Spoon rice and salmon onto serving plates; drizzle salmon with teriyaki sauce. Garnish with orange slices.

TERIYAKI CHICKEN DRUMMIES

MAKES 12 SERVINGS

1 bottle (10 ounces)
low-sodium teriyaki
sauce, divided

4 cloves garlic, crushed

¼ teaspoon black pepper

3 pounds chicken drummettes
(about 24 pieces total)

1 tablespoon toasted sesame
seeds*

*To toast sesame seeds, spread seeds in
small skillet. Shake skillet over medium-
low heat about 3 minutes or until seeds
begin to pop and turn golden.

1. Reserve ¼ cup teriyaki sauce; set aside. Combine remaining teriyaki sauce, garlic and pepper in shallow baking dish. Add drummettes; marinate in refrigerator 30 minutes, turning once.

2. Preheat oven to 400°F. Spray baking sheet with nonstick cooking spray. Remove drummettes from dish; discard marinade. Place drummettes, skin side up, on prepared baking sheet.

3. Bake 30 minutes or until golden brown. Immediately remove drummettes to large bowl. Add reserved ¼ cup teriyaki sauce; toss to coat evenly. Sprinkle with sesame seeds.

STIR-FRY CUPS

MAKES 6 CUPS

1 package (10 ounces) frozen puff pastry shells

1 bag (21 ounces) frozen vegetable stir-fry mix with teriyaki sauce

1 package (6 ounces) cooked diced chicken breast

1. Bake pastry shells according to package directions.

2. Meanwhile, prepare stir-fry mix according to package directions. Add chicken; cook and stir until heated through.

3. Spoon stir-fry mixture into prepared pastry shells, allowing some of the mixture to spill over the side.

VARIATION: To make this meal even simpler, use chicken stir-fry mix. Sprinkle sliced almonds on top to dress it up and add flavor.

SESAME CHICKEN

MAKES 4 SERVINGS

1 pound boneless skinless chicken breasts or thighs, cut into 1-inch pieces

⅔ cup teriyaki sauce, divided

2 teaspoons cornstarch

1 tablespoon peanut or vegetable oil

2 cloves garlic, minced

2 green onions, cut into ½-inch slices

1 tablespoon sesame seeds, toasted*

1 teaspoon dark sesame oil

*To toast sesame seeds, spread seeds in small skillet. Shake skillet over medium-low heat 3 minutes or until seeds begin to pop and turn golden.

1. Toss chicken with ⅓ cup teriyaki sauce in medium bowl. Marinate 15 to 20 minutes in refrigerator.

2. Drain chicken; discard marinade. Blend remaining ⅓ cup teriyaki sauce into cornstarch in small bowl until smooth.

3. Heat oil in wok or large skillet over medium-high heat. Add chicken and garlic; stir-fry 3 minutes or until chicken is cooked through. Stir cornstarch mixture; add to wok. Cook and stir 1 minute or until sauce boils and thickens. Stir in green onions, sesame seeds and sesame oil.

FRAGRANT BEEF WITH GARLIC SAUCE

MAKES 4 SERVINGS

1 boneless beef top sirloin steak (about 1¼ pounds)

⅓ cup teriyaki sauce

10 cloves garlic, peeled

½ cup beef broth

4 cups hot cooked rice (optional)

1. Place beef in large resealable food storage bag. Pour teriyaki sauce over beef. Seal bag and turn to coat beef. Marinate in refrigerator at least 30 minutes or up to 4 hours.

2. Combine garlic and broth in small saucepan. Bring to a boil over high heat. Reduce heat to medium. Simmer, uncovered, 5 minutes. Cover and simmer 8 to 9 minutes until garlic is softened. Transfer to blender or food processor; process until smooth.

3. Meanwhile, drain beef; reserve marinade. Place beef on rack of broiler pan. Brush with half of reserved marinade. Broil 5 to 6 inches from heat 6 minutes. Turn beef over; brush with remaining marinade. Broil 6 minutes more.*

4. Slice beef thinly; serve with garlic sauce and rice, if desired.

Broiling time is for medium-rare doneness. Adjust time for desired doneness.

WARM SALMON SALAD

MAKES 4 SERVINGS

Chive Vinaigrette (recipe follows)

2 cups water

¼ cup chopped onion

2 tablespoons red wine vinegar

¼ teaspoon black pepper

1¼ pounds small unpeeled red potatoes

1 pound salmon steaks

6 cups torn washed mixed salad greens

2 medium tomatoes, cut into wedges

16 pitted kalamata olives, sliced

1. Prepare Chive Vinaigrette; refrigerate until ready to use.

2. Combine water, onion, vinegar and black pepper in large saucepan; bring to a boil over medium-high heat. Add potatoes. Reduce heat to medium-low; cover and cook 10 minutes or until fork-tender. Transfer potatoes to cutting board with slotted spoon; cool slightly. Reserve water in saucepan.

3. Cut potatoes into thick slices; place in medium bowl. Toss with ⅓ cup Chive Vinaigrette.

4. Rinse salmon and pat dry with paper towels. To poach fish, place in reserved water and simmer gently 4 to 5 minutes or until fish is opaque and begins to flake easily when tested with fork. *Do not boil.* Carefully remove fish to cutting board with slotted spatula. Let stand 5 minutes; remove skin and bones. Cut fish into 1-inch pieces.

5. Divide salad greens among 4 plates; top with fish, potatoes, tomatoes and olives. Drizzle with remaining Chive Vinaigrette.

CHIVE VINAIGRETTE

MAKES ABOUT ²/₃ CUP

- ⅓ **cup vegetable oil**
- ¼ **cup red wine vinegar**
- 2 **tablespoons finely chopped fresh chives**
- 2 **tablespoons finely chopped fresh parsley**
- ⅛ **teaspoon salt**
- ⅛ **teaspoon white pepper**

Combine oil, vinegar, chives, parsley, salt and white pepper in jar with tight-fitting lid; shake well to combine.

JUST ADD

SEVERAL INGREDIENTS AND
YOU'RE GOOD TO GO

FRIENDSHIP SOUP MIX

MAKES 1 (1-QUART) JAR

⅓ cup beef bouillon granules

¼ cup dried minced onion

½ cup dried green or yellow split peas

¼ cup uncooked wild rice

⅓ cup uncooked long-grain white rice

½ cup dried red or brown lentils

½ cup uncooked elbow macaroni

1 to 1¼ cups uncooked tri-colored corkscrew pasta (or enough to fill jar)

1. Layer ingredients in order listed in 1-quart wide-mouth jar with tight-fitting lid. Pack down firmly after each layer. Seal jar.

2. Prepare Friendship Soup by following the instructions listed below.

FRIENDSHIP SOUP

MAKES 12 SERVINGS

1 jar Friendship Soup Mix

6 cups water

6 cups reduced-sodium vegetable stock or broth

2 to 3 teaspoons black pepper

½ to 1 pound ground beef or turkey, browned and drained (optional)

1. Remove pasta from jar; set aside.

2. Combine water and stock in large saucepan; bring to a boil over high heat. Add remaining contents of jar; return to a boil. Reduce heat to low; cover and simmer 20 to 30 minutes or until rice, lentils and split peas are tender.

3. Add pasta, pepper and ground beef, if desired, to saucepan; bring to a boil over high heat, stirring occasionally. Reduce heat to low; cover and simmer 10 to 12 minutes or until pasta is almost tender.

COCOA-COVERED NUT CLUSTERS MIX

MAKES 1 (1-QUART) JAR

½ **cup sugar**

¼ **teaspoon salt**

6 **tablespoons unsweetened cocoa powder**

½ **teaspoon ground cinnamon**

1½ **cups walnut halves**

¾ **cup macadamia nuts, blanched hazelnuts or whole raw almonds**

1¼ **cups pecan halves**

1. Layer ingredients in 1-quart food storage jar with tight-fitting lid in following order: sugar, salt, cocoa, cinnamon, walnuts; macadamia nuts and pecans.

2. Prepare Cocoa-Covered Nut Clusters by following the instructions listed below.

COCOA-COVERED NUT CLUSTERS

MAKES 15 SERVINGS

2 **egg whites, at room temperature**

1 **jar Cocoa-Covered Nut Clusters Mix**

1. Preheat oven to 250°F. Cover baking sheet with parchment paper.

2. Beat egg whites in large non-aluminum bowl until foamy. Add Cocoa-Covered Nut Clusters Mix; mix with wooden spoon until the cocoa mixture is wet and the nuts are coated.

3. Spread nut mixture on baking sheet. Bake 30 minutes, stirring mixture every 10 minutes. Cool completely on baking sheet on wire rack. Break into small clusters.

NOTE: Refrigerate leftover nut clusters in a container with a tight-fitting lid.

QUICK & EASY COUSCOUS MIX

MAKES 1 (1-PINT) JAR

1 cup uncooked couscous

¼ cup dried cranberries

¼ cup currants

2 tablespoons dried vegetable flakes, soup greens or dehydrated vegetables*

1 tablespoon dried minced onion

1 tablespoon dried parsley flakes

1 teaspoon chicken bouillon granules

¾ teaspoon curry powder

½ teaspoon salt

½ teaspoon black pepper

¼ teaspoon ground turmeric

¼ cup toasted slivered almonds**

*Available in the spice section of large supermarkets or in the bulk food section of natural or bulk food stores.
**To toast almonds, spread in single layer in heavy-bottomed skillet. Cook over medium heat 1 to 2 minutes, stirring frequently, until nuts are lightly browned. Remove from skillet immediately. Cool before using.*

1. Layer ½ cup couscous, cranberries, currants, vegetable flakes, dried onion, parsley flakes, bouillon granules, curry powder, salt, pepper, turmeric and remaining ½ cup couscous in 1-pint wide-mouth jar with tight-fitting lid. Place almonds in small food storage bag; add to jar. Seal jar.

2. Prepare Quick & Easy Couscous by following the instructions listed below.

QUICK & EASY COUSCOUS

MAKES 4 TO 5 SERVINGS

1 jar Quick & Easy Couscous Mix

1½ cups water

1 tablespoon butter

1. Remove almond packet from jar; set aside.

2. Place water, butter and remaining contents of jar in large saucepan. Bring to a boil. Remove pan from heat; cover and let stand 5 minutes.

3. Fluff couscous with fork; stir in almonds.

SUPER OATMEAL MIX

MAKES 1 (1-QUART) JAR

- ⅓ **cup lightly packed dark brown sugar**
- ½ **teaspoon ground cinnamon**
- ½ **teaspoon salt**
- ¼ **cup flaxseeds**
- 2¾ **cups old-fashioned oats, divided**
- ½ **cup finely diced dried figs***

- ⅓ **to ½ cup sliced almonds****

Beige Turkish figs are preferred if your market carries them.
**For more flavor, toast almonds; spread in single layer in heavy-bottomed skillet. Cook over medium heat 1 to 2 minutes, stirring frequently, until almonds are lightly browned. Remove from skillet immediately. Cool before using.*

1. Combine brown sugar, cinnamon and salt in small bowl. Stir well. Pour into 1-quart wide-mouth jar with tight-fitting lid and pack down. Add flaxseeds, 1¼ cups oats, figs, remaining 1½ cups oats and almonds. Pack down lightly after each layer. Seal jar.

2. Prepare Super Oatmeal by following the instructions listed below.

SUPER OATMEAL

MAKES 5 TO 6 SERVINGS

- 1 **jar Super Oatmeal Mix**

- 2 **cups reduced-fat (2%) or whole milk**

1. Bring 2 cups water to a boil over high heat in large heavy-bottomed saucepan. Stir in contents of jar. Immediately add 2 cups milk. Stir well.

2. Reduce heat to medium-high. Cook and stir 5 to 7 minutes or until oatmeal is thick and creamy. Spoon into individual bowls. Serve with additional milk, if desired.

RIPE BANANA MUFFIN MIX

MAKES 1 (1-QUART) JAR

2 cups whole wheat flour	1 teaspoon baking powder
¾ cup wheat bran (not bran cereal flakes)	½ teaspoon salt
½ cup wheat germ	¾ cup raw sugar
2 teaspoons ground cinnamon	¾ cup chopped walnuts
1½ teaspoons baking soda	¾ cup chocolate chips
	⅓ cup raisins

1. Whisk together flour, bran, wheat germ, cinnamon, baking soda, baking powder and salt in medium bowl. Layer into 1-quart jar with tight-fitting lid a third at a time, packing down firmly before adding next layer. Layer remaining ingredients in jar in the following order: raw sugar, walnuts, chocolate chips and raisins, packing down firmly before adding next layer.

2. Prepare Ripe Banana Muffins by following the instructions listed below.

RIPE BANANA MUFFINS

MAKES 1 DOZEN MUFFINS

1 jar Ripe Banana Muffin Mix	3 tablespoons corn or vegetable oil
1½ to 1⅔ cups very ripe mashed bananas (3 large or 4 medium bananas)	1 teaspoon vanilla
1 cup plain yogurt	1 teaspoon imitation banana extract
1 egg, beaten	

1. Preheat oven to 350°F. Spray 12-cup muffin pan with nonstick cooking spray or line with paper baking cups.

2. Whisk together contents of jar in medium bowl. Place bananas, yogurt, egg, oil, vanilla and banana extract in large bowl; stir to blend thoroughly. Add dry ingredients; stir just until moist.

3. Spoon evenly into prepared muffin cups, about ½ cup batter per muffin cup. Bake 18 to 20 minutes or until toothpick inserted into center of muffin comes out clean. Cool in pan on wire rack 5 minutes; remove from pan and cool completely on wire rack.

NUTTY ORZO AND RICE PILAF MIX

MAKES 1 (1-PINT) JAR

¾ **cup uncooked orzo pasta**

3 **tablespoons dried vegetable flakes, soup greens or dehydrated vegetables***

2 **teaspoons chicken bouillon granules**

½ **teaspoon dried thyme**

¼ **teaspoon black pepper**

½ **cup uncooked instant brown rice**

½ **cup chopped pecans**

Available in the spice section of large supermarkets or in the bulk food section of natural or bulk food stores.

1. Layer orzo, vegetable flakes, bouillon granules, thyme, pepper and rice in 1-pint jar with tight-fitting lid. Place pecans in small resealable food storage bag. Seal bag and place in jar. Seal jar.

2. Prepare Nutty Orzo and Rice Pilaf by following the instructions listed below.

NUTTY ORZO AND RICE PILAF

MAKES 4 TO 5 SERVINGS

1 **jar Nutty Orzo and Rice Pilaf Mix**

2 **cups water**

1 **tablespoon butter**

1. Preheat oven to 350°F. Remove pecan bag from jar; set aside.

2. Combine water, butter and pilaf mix in large saucepan; bring to a boil over high heat. Reduce heat to low; cover and simmer 10 to 15 minutes or until orzo is tender.

3. Meanwhile, spread pecans on ungreased baking sheet. Bake 5 to 8 minutes or just until nuts begin to darken.

4. Stir pecans into pilaf. Cook, uncovered, 2 to 3 minutes or until heated through.

VARIATIONS: Add 1 cup cooked peas and carrots *or* ½ cup drained canned sliced mushrooms in step 4. Heat through.

FULL O' FRUIT PANCAKE MIX

MAKES 1 (1-QUART) JAR

1 cup all-purpose flour	½ teaspoon ground cinnamon
½ cup nonfat dry milk powder	⅓ cup packed light brown sugar
2½ teaspoons baking powder	¼ cup dried cranberries
½ teaspoon baking soda	¼ cup old-fashioned oats
½ teaspoon salt	¼ cup chopped pitted dates
¾ cup whole wheat flour	¼ to ⅓ cup raisins

1. Combine all-purpose flour, milk powder, baking powder, baking soda and salt in medium bowl. Stir well. Pour into 1-quart wide-mouth jar with tight-fitting lid. Pack down well. Combine whole wheat flour and cinnamon. Add to jar and pack down. Add brown sugar, cranberries, oats, dates and raisins. Pack down lightly after each layer. Seal jar.

2. Prepare Full O' Fruit Pancakes by following the instructions listed below.

FULL O' FRUIT PANCAKES

MAKES 16 PANCAKES

1 jar Full O' Fruit Pancake Mix	1½ cups water
5 tablespoons unsalted butter	Maple syrup and/or cranberry sauce
3 eggs	

1. Pour contents of jar into large bowl. Stir until ingredients are evenly mixed.

2. Melt butter in large skillet over medium heat. Meanwhile, beat eggs in medium bowl. Stir in water and melted butter. Pour over dry ingredients. Stir with fork to mix well (*do not beat*).

3. Pour batter by ¼-cup measure into same skillet. Cook over medium heat 2 to 3 minutes on each side or until golden. Add more butter to skillet between batches, if necessary. Serve with maple syrup.

BARLEY, BACON AND MUSHROOM SOUP MIX

MAKES 1 (1-QUART) JAR

¼ **cup dried parsley flakes**

½ **teaspoon dried thyme**

½ **teaspoon black pepper**

1 **cup uncooked pearl barley (not quick-cooking)**

½ **cup dried chopped onion**

1 **package (1 ounce) dried sliced shiitake mushroom caps, broken into bite-size pieces**

1 **package (2.5 to 3 ounces) diced cooked shelf-stable bacon**

1. Combine parsley flakes, thyme and pepper in small bowl; stir well. Pour ½ cup barley, parsley mixture and onion into 1-quart wide-mouth jar with tight-fitting lid. Pack down well. Add mushrooms and remaining ½ cup barley. Pack down firmly after each layer. Add bacon package and pack down well. Seal jar.

2. Prepare Barley, Bacon and Mushroom Soup by following the instructions listed below.

BARLEY, BACON AND MUSHROOM SOUP

MAKES 12 SERVINGS

1 **jar Barley, Bacon and Mushroom Soup Mix**

1 **tablespoon vegetable oil**

1 **stalk celery, chopped**

2 **cloves garlic, minced**

12 **cups chicken broth***

2 **carrots, chopped**

Black pepper

*Or substitute chicken bouillon reconstituted with water.

1. Remove bacon package from jar.

2. Heat oil in 5- or 6-quart Dutch oven over medium-high heat. Add celery and garlic; cook and stir 3 minutes. Add bacon; cook and stir 1 minute. Add remaining contents of jar; stir well.

3. Add broth and carrots; bring to a boil over high heat. Reduce heat to low; partially cover and simmer 1 hour or until barley and mushrooms are tender. Season with pepper. Soup will thicken as it cools. Refrigerate leftovers.

DATE NUT BREAD MIX

MAKES 1 (1-QUART) JAR

2 cups all-purpose flour	½ cup packed brown sugar
1 tablespoon baking powder	1 cup chopped dates
½ teaspoon salt	1 cup toasted chopped walnuts
½ teaspoon ground cinnamon	

1. Combine flour, baking powder, salt and cinnamon in large bowl. Layer flour mixture, brown sugar, dates and walnuts in 1-quart jar with tight-fitting lid. Pack ingredients down lightly before adding each layer. Seal jar.

2. Prepare Date Nut Bread by following the instructions listed below.

DATE NUT BREAD

MAKES 1 LOAF

1 jar Date Nut Bread Mix	1¼ cups milk
¼ cup (½ stick) butter	1 egg

1. Preheat oven to 375°F. Spray 9×5-inch loaf pan with nonstick cooking spray.

2. Pour contents of jar into large bowl. Cut in butter with pastry blender or two knives until mixture resembles fine crumbs. Beat milk and egg in small bowl until well blended. Add to jar mixture; stir just until moistened. Pour into prepared pan.

3. Bake 45 to 50 minutes or until toothpick inserted into center comes out clean. Cool in pan on wire rack 10 minutes; remove from pan and cool completely on wire rack.

CHICKEN TORTILLA SOUP MIX

MAKES 1 (1-QUART) JAR

1 cup uncooked long grain white or brown rice

½ cup dried pinto beans

¼ cup dried chopped or minced onion

2 tablespoons chicken bouillon granules

2 teaspoons lemon-pepper seasoning

1 teaspoon dried cilantro

1 teaspoon sugar

½ teaspoon garlic powder

½ teaspoon ground cumin

½ teaspoon salt

2 to 2½ cups crushed tortilla chips

1. Place rice in 1-quart wide-mouth jar with tight-fitting lid. Place beans in small resealable food storage bag. Combine onion, bouillon granules, lemon-pepper seasoning, cilantro, sugar, garlic powder, cumin and salt in separate resealable food storage bag. Seal bags and place in jar. Pour in tortilla chips. Seal jar.

2. Prepare Chicken Tortilla Soup by following the instructions listed below.

CHICKEN TORTILLA SOUP

MAKES 12 SERVINGS

1 jar Chicken Tortilla Soup Mix

10 cups water

1 can (about 14 ounces) Mexican-style stewed tomatoes

1 can (4 ounces) diced mild green chiles

9 to 12 ounces boneless skinless chicken thighs

Shredded Cheddar cheese, diced avocado, chopped fresh cilantro and sliced black olives (optional)

1. Pour tortilla chips into small bowl; set aside. Remove packets from jar. Place beans in medium saucepan; add enough water to cover by 1 inch. Bring to a boil over high heat. Reduce heat to low; cover and simmer 5 minutes. Turn off heat and let stand, covered, 1 hour; drain.

2. Combine beans, 10 cups water, tomatoes and chiles in 6- to 8-quart saucepot. Bring to a boil over high heat. Reduce heat to low; cover and simmer 30 minutes. Add chicken thighs and contents of seasoning packet; simmer, covered, 30 minutes more. Remove chicken and shred.

3. Add rice; simmer, covered, 20 minutes or until tender. Return shredded chicken to soup; cook until heated through. Sprinkle each serving with tortilla chips. Garnish as desired.

WILD RICE AND BARLEY SOUP MIX

MAKES 1 (1-PINT) JAR

½ cup uncooked pearl barley

2 tablespoons beef bouillon granules

1 tablespoon dried celery flakes

1 teaspoon dried minced garlic

1 teaspoon dried basil

1 teaspoon dried oregano

1 teaspoon lemon-pepper seasoning

½ cup dried minced onion

½ cup uncooked wild rice

¼ cup imitation bacon bits

1. Place barley in 1-pint jar with tight-fitting lid. Combine bouillon granules, celery flakes, garlic, basil, oregano and lemon-pepper seasoning in small resealable food storage bag. Seal bag and place in jar. Add onion, rice and bacon bits in layers, packing down firmly before adding next layer. Seal jar.

2. Prepare Wild Rice and Barley Soup by following the instructions listed below.

WILD RICE AND BARLEY SOUP

MAKES 6 SERVINGS

1 jar Wild Rice and Barley Soup Mix

6 cups water

1. Place contents of jar in 5- to 6-quart saucepot; open and empty seasoning packet into mixture.

2. Add water; bring to a boil over high heat. Reduce heat to low; cover and simmer 1 hour or until rice is tender.

EASY WAFFLE MIX

MAKES 1 (1-PINT) JAR

1⅔ cups all-purpose flour	1½ teaspoons baking soda
⅓ cup nonfat dry milk	1½ teaspoons salt
3 tablespoons granulated sugar	½ teaspoon ground cinnamon
1½ teaspoons baking powder	⅛ teaspoon ground nutmeg

1. Stir together all ingredients in medium bowl. Pour mixture into 1-pint jar with tight-fitting lid one fifth at a time, packing down firmly before adding next layer.

2. Prepare Easy Waffles by following the instructions listed below.

EASY WAFFLES

MAKES 3 (9-INCH) WAFFLES

1 jar Easy Waffle Mix	1 egg
1¼ cups (10 ounces) sparkling or still water	¼ teaspoon orange extract
2 tablespoons corn or vegetable oil	

1. Preheat and prepare waffle maker according to manufacturer's instructions.

2. Place contents of jar in medium mixing bowl; add water, oil, egg and orange extract. Stir with wire whisk or fork until most lumps are gone. Let mix rest for 5 minutes.

3. Pour ⅓ batter (a generous ¾-cup portion) onto prepared waffle maker. Cook until there's no longer any steam coming from the waffle maker. Repeat with remaining batter. Serve immediately with your favorite waffle toppings.

EASY HERBED RICE MIX

- ¾ cup uncooked white or brown long-grain rice
- 2 teaspoons beef bouillon granules
- 1 teaspoon dried chopped or minced onion
- 1 teaspoon dried parsley flakes
- ½ teaspoon dried basil
- ½ teaspoon dried marjoram
- ¼ teaspoon dried minced garlic
- ¼ teaspoon salt

1. Whisk together ingredients in small bowl. Pack in half-pint jar with tight-fitting lid.

2. Prepare Easy Herbed Rice by following the instructions listed below.

EASY HERBED RICE

MAKES ABOUT 3 CUPS

- 1 jar Easy Herbed Rice Mix
- 1½ cups water
- 1 tablespoon unsalted butter

Combine contents of jar, water and butter in medium saucepan. Bring to a boil over high heat; stir, cover, reduce heat and simmer 20 minutes. Remove from heat and let sit, covered, 15 to 20 minutes. Remove lid, fluff rice with fork and serve.

HEARTY LENTIL & BARLEY SOUP MIX

MAKES 1 (1-PINT) JAR

¾ cup dried brown or red lentils

¼ cup sun-dried tomato halves, cut into pieces

2 tablespoons dried vegetable flakes, soup greens or dehydrated vegetables*

1 tablespoon dried minced onion

2 teaspoons chicken bouillon granules

1 teaspoon dried oregano

½ teaspoon dried minced garlic

½ teaspoon black pepper

⅛ teaspoon red pepper flakes (optional)

½ cup uncooked medium pearl barley

Available in the spice section of large supermarkets or in the bulk food section of natural or bulk food stores.

1. Layer lentils, sun-dried tomatoes, vegetable flakes, onion, bouillon granules, oregano, garlic, black pepper, red pepper flakes, if desired, and barley in 1-pint food storage jar with tight-fitting lid. Seal jar.

2. Prepare Hearty Lentil & Barley Soup by following the instructions listed below.

HEARTY LENTIL & BARLEY SOUP

MAKES 10 TO 12 SERVINGS

1 jar Hearty Lentil & Barley Soup Mix

5 to 6 cups water

1 can (about 14 ounces) diced tomatoes with green pepper, celery and onion, undrained

8 ounces smoked sausage, cut into ½-inch slices

Lemon-pepper seasoning

Simmer all ingredients in Dutch oven, partially covered, 1 to 1½ hours or until lentils are tender.

SLOW COOK & GO

PREP IN THE MORNING...READY IN THE EVENING

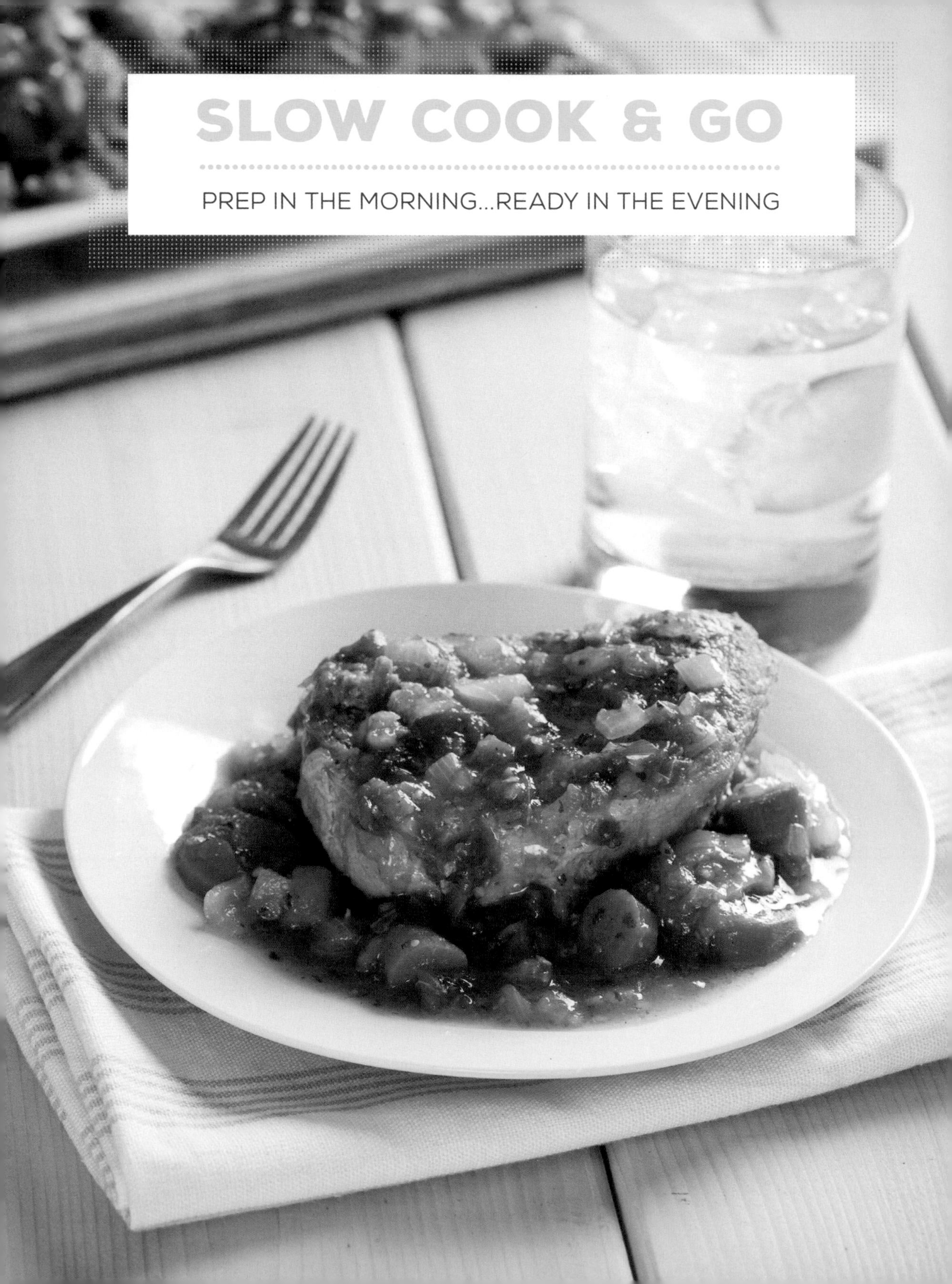

CHILI VERDE

1 tablespoon vegetable oil
1 to 2 pounds boneless pork chops
2 cups sliced carrots

1 jar (24 ounces) mild green salsa
1 cup chopped onion

1. Heat oil in large skillet over medium-low heat. Add pork; cook 3 to 5 minutes or until browned on both sides. Drain excess fat.

2. Place carrots in bottom of slow cooker. Place pork on top of carrots. Pour salsa and onion over pork. Cover; cook on HIGH 6 to 8 hours.

VARIATION: The pork can also be shredded and served in tortillas.

BEAN AND VEGETABLE BURRITOS

MAKES 4 SERVINGS

2 tablespoons chili powder

2 teaspoons dried oregano

1½ teaspoons ground cumin

1 large sweet potato, diced

1 can (about 15 ounces) black or pinto beans, rinsed and drained

4 cloves garlic, minced

1 medium onion, halved and thinly sliced

1 jalapeño pepper,* seeded and minced

1 green bell pepper, chopped

1 cup frozen corn, thawed and drained

3 tablespoons lime juice

1 tablespoon chopped fresh cilantro

¾ cup (3 ounces) shredded Monterey Jack cheese

4 (10-inch) flour tortillas

Sour cream (optional)

Jalapeño peppers can sting and irritate the skin, so wear rubber gloves when handling peppers and do not touch your eyes.

1. Combine chili powder, oregano and cumin in small bowl. Set aside.

2. Layer ingredients in slow cooker in the following order: sweet potato, beans, half of chili powder mixture, garlic, onion, jalapeño pepper, bell pepper, remaining half of chili powder mixture and corn. Cover; cook on LOW 5 hours or until sweet potato is tender. Stir in lime juice and cilantro.

3. Preheat oven to 350°F. Spoon about 2 tablespoons cheese in center of each tortilla. Top with 1 cup filling. Fold two sides over filling and roll up. Place burritos, seam side down, on baking sheet. Cover with foil and bake 20 to 30 minutes or until heated through. Serve with sour cream, if desired.

HAMBURGER VEGGIE SOUP

MAKES 4 TO 6 SERVINGS

1 pound ground beef

1 bag (16 ounces) frozen mixed vegetables

1 bag (10 ounces) frozen seasoning blend vegetables

1 can (about 14 ounces) stewed tomatoes, undrained

2 cans (5½ ounces each) spicy vegetable juice

1 can (10¾ ounces) condensed tomato soup, undiluted

Salt and black pepper

1. Brown beef in large skillet over medium-high heat 6 to 8 minutes, stirring to break up meat. Drain fat.

2. Combine beef, vegetables, tomatoes with juice, vegetable juice and soup in slow cooker. Stir well.

3. Cover; cook on HIGH 4 hours. Season with salt and pepper.

CARIBBEAN SHRIMP WITH RICE

MAKES 4 SERVINGS

1 package (12 ounces) frozen large raw shrimp, thawed (with tails on)
½ cup fat-free reduced-sodium chicken broth
1 clove garlic, minced
1 teaspoon chili powder
½ teaspoon salt
½ teaspoon dried oregano
1 cup frozen peas, thawed
½ cup diced tomatoes
2 cups cooked long grain rice

1. Combine shrimp, broth, garlic, chili powder, salt and oregano in slow cooker. Cover; cook on LOW 2 hours.

2. Add peas and tomatoes. Cover; cook on LOW 5 minutes.

3. Stir in rice. Cover; cook on LOW an additional 5 minutes.

LEMON PORK CHOPS

MAKES 4 SERVINGS

1 tablespoon vegetable oil

4 boneless pork chops

3 cans (about 8 ounces each) tomato sauce

1 onion, quartered and sliced (optional)

1 green bell pepper, cut into strips

1 tablespoon lemon-pepper seasoning

1 tablespoon Worcestershire sauce

3 lemons, quartered, divided

1. Heat oil in large skillet over medium heat. Brown pork chops on both sides. Transfer to slow cooker.

2. Combine tomato sauce, onion, if desired, bell pepper, lemon-pepper seasoning and Worcestershire sauce in medium bowl. Add to slow cooker.

3. Squeeze juice from 4 lemon quarters over mixture; place squeezed lemon quarters into slow cooker. Cover; cook on LOW 6 to 8 hours. Remove and discard cooked lemon before serving. Serve pork with remaining lemon quarters.

SERVING SUGGESTION: These pork chops are great served with green beans and couscous.

SPRING VEGETABLE RAGOÛT

MAKES 6 SERVINGS

1 tablespoon olive oil

2 leeks, thinly sliced

3 cloves garlic, minced

1 cup vegetable broth

1 package (10 ounces) frozen corn

½ pound yellow squash, halved lengthwise and cut into ½-inch pieces (about 1¼ cups)

1 small bag (6 ounces) frozen edamame (soybeans), shelled

1 small bag (4 ounces) shredded carrots

3 cups small cherry tomatoes, halved

1 teaspoon dried tarragon

1 teaspoon dried basil

1 teaspoon dried oregano

Salt and black pepper (optional)

Minced fresh parsley (optional)

1. Heat oil in large skillet over medium heat. Add leeks and garlic; cook and stir just until fragrant.

2. Combine leeks and garlic with broth, corn, squash, edamame, carrots, tomatoes, tarragon, basil and oregano in slow cooker; stir well. Cover; cook on LOW 6 to 8 hours or on HIGH 3 to 4 hours or until vegetables are tender.

3. Season with salt and pepper, if desired. Garnish with parsley.

HOT THREE-BEAN CASSEROLE

MAKES 12 SERVINGS

2 tablespoons olive oil

1 cup coarsely chopped onion

1 cup chopped celery

2 cloves garlic, minced

2½ cups (10 ounces) frozen cut green beans

1 can (about 15 ounces) chickpeas, rinsed and drained

1 can (about 15 ounces) kidney beans, rinsed and drained

1 cup coarsely chopped tomato

1 cup water

1 can (about 8 ounces) tomato sauce

1 to 2 jalapeño peppers,* minced

1 tablespoon chili powder

2 teaspoons sugar

1½ teaspoons ground cumin

1 teaspoon salt

1 teaspoon dried oregano

¼ teaspoon black pepper

Fresh oregano (optional)

*Jalapeño peppers can sting and irritate the skin, so wear rubber gloves when handling peppers and do not touch your eyes.

1. Heat oil in large skillet over medium heat. Add onion, celery and garlic; cook and stir 5 minutes or until tender.

2. Combine onion mixture and remaining ingredients in slow cooker. Cover; cook on LOW 6 to 8 hours. Garnish with fresh oregano, if desired.

SHRIMP LOUISIANA-STYLE

MAKES 3 TO 4 SERVINGS

1 **pound raw medium to large shrimp, unpeeled, rinsed (with tails on)**

½ **cup (1 stick) butter, diced**

⅓ **cup lemon juice**

1 **tablespoon Worcestershire sauce**

1 **teaspoon minced garlic**

1 **teaspoon seafood seasoning**

½ **teaspoon salt**

½ **teaspoon coarsely ground black pepper**

1½ **teaspoons grated lemon peel, plus additional for garnish**

Hot cooked rice (optional)

4 **lemon wedges (optional)**

1. Coat slow cooker with nonstick cooking spray. Place shrimp in bottom. Add butter, lemon juice, Worcestershire sauce, garlic, seafood seasoning, salt and pepper. Stir well to combine. Cover; cook on HIGH 1 hour and 15 minutes.

2. Turn off slow cooker. Stir in 1½ teaspoons lemon peel. Let stand, uncovered, 5 minutes. Serve in shallow soup bowls over rice, if desired. Garnish with additional grated lemon peel and serve with lemon wedges.

CHUNKY CHILI

MAKES 4 (1½-CUP) SERVINGS

1 pound 90% lean ground beef

1 medium onion, chopped

2 cans (about 14 ounces each) diced tomatoes, undrained

1 can (about 15 ounces) pinto beans, rinsed and drained

½ cup salsa

1 tablespoon chili powder

1½ teaspoons ground cumin

Salt and black pepper

½ cup (2 ounces) shredded Cheddar cheese

3 tablespoons sour cream

Sliced black olives

1. Cook and stir beef and onion in large skillet at medium-high heat until beef is browned and onion is tender. Drain fat.

2. Place beef mixture, tomatoes with juice, beans, salsa, chili powder and cumin in slow cooker; stir. Cover; cook on LOW 5 to 6 hours or until flavors are blended. Season to taste with salt and pepper. Serve with cheese, sour cream and olives.

SERVING SUGGESTION: Serve with tossed green salad and corn bread muffins.

ENJOY DESSERTS

PREPARE IN A JAR OR STACK IN A DISH—
YOU'RE READY TO SERVE

BERRY SHORTCAKE TRIFLES

MAKES 4 (1-PINT) JARS

LEMON CURD

- 1 cup granulated sugar
- ½ cup (1 stick) butter
- ⅔ cup fresh lemon juice
- 1 tablespoon grated lemon peel
- ¼ teaspoon salt
- 4 eggs, beaten

BERRIES

- ½ pound fresh strawberries, stemmed and diced
- ½ pound fresh blueberries

- ⅓ cup granulated sugar

WHIPPED CREAM

- 4 ounces cream cheese, softened
- 6 tablespoons powdered sugar, divided
- 1 cup whipping cream, divided
- ¼ teaspoon vanilla

- 1 prepared pound cake (about 14 ounces), cut into ½-inch cubes

1. Combine 1 cup granulated sugar, butter, lemon juice, lemon peel and salt in medium saucepan over medium heat, stirring until butter is melted and sugar is dissolved. Gradually whisk in eggs in thin, steady stream. Cook over medium-low heat 5 minutes or until thickened to the consistency of pudding, whisking constantly. Strain through fine-mesh sieve into medium bowl. Press plastic wrap onto surface; refrigerate at least 2 hours or until cold.

2. Meanwhile, combine strawberries, blueberries and ⅓ cup granulated sugar in medium bowl. Cover and refrigerate at least 2 hours.

3. Beat cream cheese, 3 tablespoons powdered sugar, 2 tablespoons whipping cream and vanilla in large bowl with electric mixer on medium speed 3 minutes or until smooth. In separate bowl, beat remaining whipping cream and remaining 3 tablespoons powdered sugar to stiff peaks with electric mixer on high speed. Fold into cream cheese mixture until well blended.

4. Drain berries, reserving juice. Place ½ cup pound cake cubes in each of 4 wide-mouth (1-pint) jars. Sprinkle cake cubes in each jar with 3 teaspoons reserved juice. Top with scant ¼ cup whipped cream, 2 tablespoons lemon curd and 1 tablespoon berries. Repeat layers. Refrigerate overnight.

HALLOWEEN PUDDING CUPS

MAKES 5 SERVINGS

1 box (about 18 ounces)
   brownie mix, plus
   ingredients to prepare mix
1 package (4-serving size)
   instant vanilla pudding mix,
   plus ingredients to prepare
   or 4 single-serving vanilla
   pudding cups

Orange food coloring
Chocolate sprinkles

1. Grease 9×13-inch square baking pan. Bake and cool brownies according to package directions.

2. Meanwhile, prepare pudding according to package directions. Once pudding reaches desired consistency, add food coloring, 2 to 3 drops at a time, until desired shade of orange is reached.

3. Once brownies cool, remove from pan. Cut 15 circles using 2-inch circle cutter. Place 1 brownie circle in bottom of 5 (2-inch diameter) glasses or jars. Top with 1 to 2 tablespoon orange pudding. Repeat layers twice to fill glass. Top with chocolate sprinkles. Repeat with remaining glasses.

TIP: These layered treats can also be built in small shot glasses or other small glasses. Cut the brownies slightly smaller than the width of the glass or jar and stack to desired height.

MANGO VANILLA PARFAIT

MAKES 2 SERVINGS

½ (4-serving size) package vanilla instant pudding and pie filling mix

1¼ cups milk

½ cup cubed mango

2 large strawberries, sliced

3 sugar-free shortbread cookies, crumbled *or* 2 tablespoons reduced-fat granola

Strawberry slices (optional)

1. Prepare pudding according to package directions using 1¼ cups milk.

2. Layer one quarter of pudding, half of mango, half of strawberries and one quarter of pudding in parfait glass or small glass bowl. Repeat layers in second parfait glass. Refrigerate 30 minutes.

3. Just before serving, top with cookie crumbs and garnish with strawberries.

BROWNIE ICE CREAM TREATS

MAKES 8 (½-CUP) SERVINGS

½ cup all-purpose flour

½ teaspoon salt

¼ teaspoon baking powder

6 tablespoons (¾ stick) butter

1 cup sugar

½ cup unsweetened Dutch process cocoa powder

2 eggs

½ teaspoon vanilla

8 (2¼-inch) jars with lids

2 cups pistachio or any flavor ice cream, slightly softened

Hot fudge topping, heated (optional)

1. Preheat oven to 350°F. Spray 9-inch square baking pan with nonstick cooking spray. Combine flour, salt and baking powder in small bowl; stir to blend.

2. Melt butter in medium saucepan over low heat. Stir in sugar until blended. Stir in cocoa until well blended. Stir in eggs, one at a time, then vanilla. Stir in flour mixture until blended. Pour into prepared pan.

3. Bake 20 minutes or until toothpick inserted into center comes out with fudgy crumbs. Cool completely in pan on wire rack.

4. For 2¼-inch-wide jars, cut out 16 brownies using 2-inch round cookie or biscuit cutter. (See Tip.) Remove brownie scraps from pan (any pieces left between round cut-outs); crumble into small pieces. Save remaining brownies for another use.

5. Place one brownie in each of 8 (½-cup) glass jars. Top with 2 tablespoons ice cream, pressing to form flat layer over brownie. Repeat brownie and ice cream layers.

6. Drizzle with hot fudge topping, if desired, and sprinkle with brownie crumbs. Serve immediately or make ahead through step 5. Cover and freeze until ready to serve.

STRAWBERRY CHEESECAKE DESSERT SHOOTERS

MAKES 8 TO 10 SERVINGS

1 cup graham cracker crumbs, plus additional for garnish

¼ cup (½ stick) butter, melted

2 cups chopped fresh strawberries

¾ cup sugar, divided

12 ounces cream cheese, softened

2 eggs

2 tablespoons sour cream

½ teaspoon vanilla

Whipped cream

1. Place 1 cup graham cracker crumbs in medium nonstick skillet; cook and stir over medium heat about 3 minutes or until lightly browned. Transfer to small bowl; stir in butter until well blended. Press mixture evenly into 8 to 10 (3- to 4-ounce) shot glasses.

2. Combine strawberries and ¼ cup sugar in small bowl; toss to coat. Cover and refrigerate until ready to serve.

3. Beat cream cheese in medium bowl with electric mixer at medium speed until creamy. Add eggs, remaining ½ cup sugar, sour cream and vanilla; beat until well blended. Transfer to medium saucepan; cook over medium heat 5 to 6 minutes or until thickened and smooth, stirring frequently. Divide filling evenly among prepared crusts. Refrigerate 1 hour or until cold.

4. Top each serving with strawberries and whipped cream. Garnish with additional graham cracker crumbs.

TIP: For larger servings, use 4 to 5 (6- or 8-ounce) juice or stemless wine glasses. Divide crumb mixture, filling and strawberries evenly among glasses.

BROWNIE LAYER DESSERT IN A JAR

MAKES 4 (1-PINT) JARS

1 package (19 to 21 ounces) chocolate brownie mix, plus ingredients to prepare

1 package (4-serving size) chocolate instant pudding mix, plus ingredients to prepare

2 cups powdered sugar

1 package (4 ounces) cream cheese, softened

1 to 2 teaspoons milk

¼ teaspoon vanilla

1 cup mini chocolate chips, divided

½ of an 8-ounce container frozen whipped topping, thawed

1. Prepare brownie mix according to package directions for 13×9-inch pan. Cool completely.

2. Prepare pudding mix according to package directions; set aside.

3. Combine powdered sugar, cream cheese, milk and vanilla in medium bowl; beat with electric mixer at medium speed 1 to 2 minutes or until creamy. Fold in chocolate chips. Set aside.

4. Cut cooled brownies into 8 (3-inch) circles (or size of jar). Layer in 4 (1-pint) jars in the following order: 1 brownie circle, ¼ cup cream cheese filling, ½ cup pudding filling, 1 brownie circle and whipping topping.

5. Refrigerate until ready to serve.

KEY LIME MINIS

MAKES 4 (1/2-PINT) JARS

6 **whole graham crackers**
2 **tablespoons butter**
  Pinch of salt
1 **tablespoon whipping cream
  or milk**
1 **can (14 ounces) sweetened
  condensed milk**

6 **tablespoons key lime juice**
3 **egg yolks**
1 **drop** *each* **yellow and green
  food coloring**
  Whipped topping (optional)
  Lime slices (optional)

1. Place graham crackers in food processor; pulse until coarse crumbs form. Add butter, salt and cream; pulse until well blended.

2. Whisk sweetened condensed milk, lime juice, egg yolks and food coloring in medium saucepan. Cook over medium-low heat 5 to 7 minutes, whisking frequently. Remove from heat; cool 10 minutes.

3. Press 2 heaping tablespoons crumb mixture into bottom of 4 (1/2-pint) jars. Top evenly with lime mixture.

4. Refrigerate overnight. Top with whipped topping and lime slices, as desired.

RASPBERRY BROWNIE PUDDING PARFAIT

MAKES 8 SERVINGS

1 package (6-serving size) vanilla cook-and-serve pudding and pie filling mix

½ cup white chocolate chips

1 pan (8-inch-square) prepared brownies

½ cup raspberry jam

1 pint fresh raspberries

Whipped topping (optional)

1. Prepare pudding according to package directions. Remove pan from heat; immediately stir in white chocolate chips until melted and smooth. Place pudding in small bowl; cover and chill 2 hours.

2. Cut brownies into ½-inch cubes. Layer brownie cubes, pudding, jam and raspberries in 8 parfait glasses. Top with whipped topping, if desired.

TIP: Homemade brownies or brownies prepared from a mix can also be used in these parfaits. Or, substitute your favorite cookies, broken into chunks.

S'MORES IN A JAR

MAKES 8 (1/2-PINT) JARS

CRUST

1 sleeve honey graham crackers (9 whole crackers)
1/4 cup (1/2 stick) butter, melted
1/4 teaspoon salt

CHOCOLATE MOUSSE

1 cup semisweet chocolate chips
2 cups chilled whipping cream, divided

4 egg yolks
Pinch of salt
1 teaspoon vanilla
1/4 cup granulated sugar

MARSHMALLOW TOPPING

1 jar (7 ounces) marshmallow creme
1 cup mini marshmallows

1. For crust, place graham crackers in food processor; process until coarse crumbs form. Add butter and 1/4 teaspoon salt; process until blended. Press 2 tablespoons mixture into each of 8 wide-mouth (1/2-pint) jars. Freeze 10 minutes.

2. Heat chocolate chips in medium saucepan over low heat until melted, stirring frequently. Remove from heat and stir in 1/4 cup whipping cream.

3. Place egg yolks and pinch of salt in medium bowl. Whisk about half of chocolate mixture into egg yolks; whisk egg yolk mixture back into chocolate mixture in saucepan. Cook over low heat 2 minutes, whisking constantly. Remove from heat; cool 5 minutes.

4. Beat remaining 1¾ cups whipping cream and vanilla to soft peaks in medium bowl. Gradually beat in sugar; continue beating until stiff peaks form. Stir about one fourth of whipped cream into chocolate mixture; fold chocolate mixture into remaining whipped cream until completely combined.

5. Scoop heaping spoonful of marshmallow creme on top of crust in each jar. Press into even layer with dampened hands. Top with heaping 1/4 cup mousse.

6. For garnish, preheat broiler. Spray small baking pan with nonstick cooking spray. Spread marshmallows in prepared pan. Broil about 30 seconds or until marshmallows are toasted. Scoop toasted marshmallows on top of each serving; sprinkle with additional graham cracker mixture, if desired.

BIRTHDAY CAKE IN A JAR

MAKES 20 (1-PINT) JARS

CAKE

- 2 cups all-purpose flour
- 4 teaspoons baking powder
- ½ teaspoon salt
- 1½ cups granulated sugar
- ½ cup (1 stick) butter, softened
- 1 cup milk
- 1 teaspoon vanilla
- 3 eggs
- ½ cup rainbow sprinkles

FROSTING

- ½ cup (1 stick) butter, softened
- 3 cups powdered sugar
- 3 tablespoons whipping cream
- ½ teaspoon vanilla

GARNISHES

Ice cream

Chocolate ice cream topping

Additional sprinkles

1. Preheat oven to 350°F. Spray jelly-roll pan with nonstick cooking spray; line with parchment paper.

2. Sift flour, baking powder and salt in large bowl. Stir in granulated sugar. Add ½ cup butter, milk and 1 teaspoon vanilla; beat with electric mixer on low speed 30 seconds. Beat on medium speed 2 minutes. Add eggs; beat 2 minutes. Fold in ½ cup sprinkles. Pour into prepared pan.

3. Bake 18 to 20 minutes or until toothpick inserted into center comes out clean. Cool completely in pan on wire rack.

4. For frosting, beat ½ cup butter in large bowl on medium speed 30 seconds or until creamy. Gradually add powdered sugar alternately with whipping cream; add ½ teaspoon vanilla. Beat on medium-high speed until light and fluffy.

5. Cut cake in half crosswise. Spread half of frosting over one cake half; top with remaining cake. Spread remaining frosting over top of cake; sprinkle with additional sprinkles.

6. Cut cake into circles or squares that will fit into 1-pint jars; place one cake circle into each jar. Top with scoop of ice cream, chocolate ice cream topping and additional sprinkles, as desired.

APPLE TRIFLE IN A JAR

MAKES 3 (1-PINT) SERVINGS

1 cup milk

1 tablespoon cornstarch

3 tablespoons packed dark brown sugar

⅛ teaspoon salt

2 eggs

1 tablespoon butter

1 teaspoon vanilla

½ teaspoon rum extract

½ cup apple cider, divided

¼ cup raisins

1 teaspoon ground cinnamon

2 cups peeled and chopped Fuji apples (2 apples)

½ angel food cake, cut into cubes and divided

1. To prepare custard, combine milk and cornstarch in small, heavy saucepan; stir until cornstarch is completely dissolved. Add brown sugar, salt, eggs and butter; blend well. Slowly bring to a boil over medium-low heat until thickened, about 5 minutes, stirring constantly with whisk. Remove from heat; stir in vanilla and rum extract. Set aside; cool completely.

2. Combine ¼ cup apple cider, raisins and cinnamon in medium saucepan; bring to a boil over medium-low heat. Add apple; cook until apple is fork-tender and all liquid has been absorbed, stirring frequently. Remove from heat; set aside to cool.

3. Place cake cubes in medium bowl. Sprinkle with remaining ¼ cup apple cider; toss to coat.

4. To assemble jars, place ¼ cup cake cubes in bottom of 6 (1-pint) jars. Spoon custard mixture over cake. Top with apple mixture. Repeat layers. Refrigerate until ready to serve.

PUMPKIN MOUSSE CUPS

MAKES 8 (¹/₂-CUP) SERVINGS

1¼ cups whipping cream, divided

1 cup canned pumpkin

⅓ cup sugar

½ teaspoon pumpkin pie spice

⅛ teaspoon salt

½ teaspoon vanilla

½ cup crushed gingersnap cookies (about 8 small gingersnaps)

1. Combine ½ cup whipping cream, pumpkin, sugar, pumpkin pie spice and salt in small saucepan; bring to a simmer over medium heat. Reduce heat to low; simmer 15 minutes, stirring occasionally. Remove from heat; stir in vanilla. Set aside to cool to room temperature.

2. Beat remaining ¾ cup whipping cream in medium bowl with electric mixer at high speed until soft peaks form. Gently fold 1 cup whipped cream into pumpkin mixture until well blended. Refrigerate until ready to serve.

3. Spoon heaping ¼ cup pumpkin mousse into each of 8 (½-cup) glasses or dessert dishes. Top with dollop of remaining whipped cream; sprinkle with crushed cookies.

TIP: Store leftover canned pumpkin in an airtight container in the refrigerator for up to 1 week or in the freezer for up to 3 months.

PETITE PUDDING PARFAITS

MAKES ABOUT 8 SERVINGS

2 ounces bittersweet or semisweet chocolate, chopped (or about ⅓ cup chips)

2 ounces white chocolate, chopped (or about ⅓ cup chips)

½ cup sugar

2 tablespoons all-purpose flour

1 tablespoon cornstarch

⅛ teaspoon salt

2¼ cups milk

2 egg yolks, beaten

2 teaspoons vanilla

8 (2-ounce) shot glasses

Chocolate curls or grated bittersweet chocolate (optional)

1. Place bittersweet chocolate and white chocolate in separate heatproof bowls; set aside.

2. Combine sugar, flour, cornstarch and salt in small saucepan. Gradually whisk in milk. Cook over medium heat, stirring constantly, until mixture comes to a boil. Boil 2 minutes, stirring constantly.

3. Remove saucepan from heat. Drizzle small amount of hot mixture into beaten egg yolks, stirring constantly. Stir egg yolk mixture into saucepan; cook and stir over low heat until thickened. Remove from heat; stir in vanilla.

4. Spoon half of egg yolk mixture over each chocolate; stir until chocolates are completely melted.

5. Alternate layers of puddings in shot glasses using about 1 tablespoon pudding for each layer. Cover and refrigerate until chilled. Top with chocolate curls before serving, if desired.

CHOCOLATE PEPPERMINT JARS

MAKES 6 (½-PINT) SERVINGS

18 chocolate sandwich
cookies, finely crushed
(about 1½ cups)

1 pint peppermint ice cream

½ container frozen whipped
topping, thawed

Crushed peppermint candies
(optional)

1. Layer 2 tablespoons crushed cookies in bottom of 6 (½-pint) jars. Top with 2 tablespoons ice cream. Repeat layers.

2. Top with whipped topping and crushed candies, if desired.

INDEX

METRIC CONVERSION CHART

VOLUME MEASUREMENTS (dry)

1/8 teaspoon = 0.5 mL
1/4 teaspoon = 1 mL
1/2 teaspoon = 2 mL
3/4 teaspoon = 4 mL
1 teaspoon = 5 mL
1 tablespoon = 15 mL
2 tablespoons = 30 mL
1/4 cup = 60 mL
1/3 cup = 75 mL
1/2 cup = 125 mL
2/3 cup = 150 mL
3/4 cup = 175 mL
1 cup = 250 mL
2 cups = 1 pint = 500 mL
3 cups = 750 mL
4 cups = 1 quart = 1 L

VOLUME MEASUREMENTS (fluid)

1 fluid ounce (2 tablespoons) = 30 mL
4 fluid ounces (1/2 cup) = 125 mL
8 fluid ounces (1 cup) = 250 mL
12 fluid ounces (1 1/2 cups) = 375 mL
16 fluid ounces (2 cups) = 500 mL

WEIGHTS (mass)

1/2 ounce = 15 g
1 ounce = 30 g
3 ounces = 90 g
4 ounces = 120 g
8 ounces = 225 g
10 ounces = 285 g
12 ounces = 360 g
16 ounces = 1 pound = 450 g

DIMENSIONS

1/16 inch = 2 mm
1/8 inch = 3 mm
1/4 inch = 6 mm
1/2 inch = 1.5 cm
3/4 inch = 2 cm
1 inch = 2.5 cm

OVEN TEMPERATURES

250°F = 120°C
275°F = 140°C
300°F = 150°C
325°F = 160°C
350°F = 180°C
375°F = 190°C
400°F = 200°C
425°F = 220°C
450°F = 230°C

BAKING PAN SIZES

Utensil	Size in Inches/Quarts	Metric Volume	Size in Centimeters
Baking or Cake Pan (square or rectangular)	8×8×2	2 L	20×20×5
	9×9×2	2.5 L	23×23×5
	12×8×2	3 L	30×20×5
	13×9×2	3.5 L	33×23×5
Loaf Pan	8×4×3	1.5 L	20×10×7
	9×5×3	2 L	23×13×7
Round Layer Cake Pan	8×1½	1.2 L	20×4
	9×1½	1.5 L	23×4
Pie Plate	8×1¼	750 mL	20×3
	9×1¼	1 L	23×3
Baking Dish or Casserole	1 quart	1 L	—
	1½ quart	1.5 L	—
	2 quart	2 L	—